Twisdoms about Paying for College

Mark Kantrowitz
Publisher of Edvisors.com

Twisdoms about Paying for College

ISBN: 978-0-9914646-4-7

For information, write to Edvisors Network Inc., 10000 W. Charleston Boulevard, Suite 200, Las Vegas, NV 89135.

About the Author

Mark Kantrowitz is Senior Vice President and Publisher of Edvisors.com, a comprehensive web site about planning and paying for college.

Mark is a nationally recognized expert on student financial aid, scholarships and student loans. He has testified before Congress about student aid policy on several occasions and is frequently interviewed by news outlets. He has been quoted in more than 5,000 newspaper and magazine articles in the last five years. He has written for the *New York Times, Wall Street Journal, Forbes, Washington Post, Reuters, Huffington Post, U.S. News & World Report, Newsweek* and *Time Magazine.*

Mark is the author of three bestselling books about scholarships and financial aid, including *Filing the FAFSA, Secrets to Winning a Scholarship* and *College Gold: The Step-by-Step Guide to Paying for College,* and holds seven patents. The *Filing the FAFSA* book won an Excellence in Financial Literacy Education (EIFLE) Award from the Institute for Financial Literacy.

Over his career, Mark has helped more than 100 million students and their families learn how to pay for college.

Mark is a member of the board of directors of the National Scholarship Providers Association and the board of trustees of the Center for Excellence in Education. Mark serves on the editorial board of the *Journal of Student Financial Aid* and the editorial advisory board of *Bottom Line/Personal.*

Mark was named a Money Hero by Money Magazine. He received a Special Award from the College Board and the

Jefferson Medal from the American Institute for Public Service. Mark received the President's Award from the National Association of Graduate and Professional Students and was a finalist for the Above & Beyond Citizen Honors from the Congressional Medal of Honor Society. He received the Creative Leadership Award from the California Association of Student Financial Aid Administrators (CASFAA) and the Meritorious Achievement Award from the National Association of Student Financial Aid Administrators (NASFAA).

Mark has a Master of Science degree in computer science from Carnegie Mellon University (CMU) and Bachelor of Science degrees in mathematics and philosophy from the Massachusetts Institute of Technology (MIT). He is also an alumnus of the Research Science Institute (RSI) program established by Admiral H.G. Rickover.

Acknowledgements

I would like to thank my colleagues at Edvisors, including:

- Jacob Boucon
- Mikal Calvert
- Nancy Ciccone
- Lori Crepas
- Michael Dubendris
- Len Fainer
- John Falb
- Jeff Henson
- Chris Hodge
- Eric Hutchinson
- Erin Leonardi
- David Levy
- Joanne Madore
- Michael McGowan
- Anita Myles
- Jared Norman
- Tessie Osmena
- Jon Romano
- Barbara Sharpe
- Todd Shaul
- Joe Taylor
- Russ Theriault
- Todd Transue
- Marianne Worley
- Paul Wozniak
- Jeff Zuill

Joe Taylor deserves special recognition for designing the cover of this book.

Mark Kantrowitz

Table of Contents

Foreword

By Jean Chatzky
Financial Editor, NBC Today
Author, Money Rules

As a personal finance journalist for the past 25-plus years, I like to think I've compiled one of the best Rolodexes in the business. (These days, it's largely virtual, but that's beside the point.) Whether I'm writing about how to snag a good deal on a mortgage, rebalance your portfolio or make your retirement savings last as long as you do, I know precisely who to call for the most objective, most up-to-date information.

When the topic turns to college, I call Mark Kantrowitz. Over the past two decades, Mark has made himself an indispensable resource when it comes to every aspect of paying for college – from saving to borrowing to scholarships and grants. That's why you've read his opinions and analysis (as well as his own writing) in so many of the nation's leading publications, online and off.

One of the biggest complaints about college financing of all sorts is that it's complicated. Filling out the FAFSA? Complicated. Choosing among competing aid offers? Complicated. Deciding how much to borrow, how much to pull out of savings, how much to pay out of current cash flow? Complicated. Complicated. Complicated.

With the launch of *Twisdoms about Paying for College*, Kantrowitz is forging a path of clarity. He is taking these complicated issues and boiling them down into no more than 140 characters and in doing so, presenting readers with a way to look at many of the college-financing decisions they're asked to make and being able to say "yes" or "no." When I wrote my book, Money Rules: The Simple Path to Lifelong Security, I took a similar approach. My thesis was that a life without rules – whether we're talking about traffic rules or stock trading rules – is, ultimately, chaotic. It's also unnecessary. Kantrowitz, based upon his years of experience, research and accumulated knowledge, is able to give us lines in which to color. He's able to give us guidelines to which we should adhere. And, with Twisdoms, he's able to do it over and over again, in a straightforward, easy-to-remember way.

"Scholarships are part of the plan for paying for college but not the entire plan," he writes.

"Borrowing excessive student loans can be like having a mortgage without owning a home."

"The main problem is the *amount* of debt not the *cost* of debt."

And my favorite: "Student loan debt is like cooking a lobster. By the time you notice that the water is boiling you are already cooked."

Shortly after Money Rules was published, an early reader commented that it was a great "bathroom book." Not only did I decide not to take offense at that, I decided to take it as a compliment. A great bathroom book is a book that you can pick up and put down over and over again – getting something valuable out of it each time, whether you peruse one page or many.

Twisdoms is precisely this type of read. I plan to keep it on my Kindle where I can dip into and out of it at my leisure, for many years to come.

What is a Twisdom?

A twisdom is a tweetable wisdom, a short quotable quote that conveys practical advice, such as a strategy or actionable rule of thumb.

Examples of twisdoms include:

- Live like a student while you are in school, so you don't have to live like a student after you graduate.
- Student loan debt is like cooking a lobster. By the time you notice the water is boiling, you are already cooked.
- Warning: Cosigning a student loan may be hazardous to your wealth.

This book compiles a collection of more than 400 twisdoms about paying for college, written by Mark Kantrowitz over the last several decades. Each rule of thumb is written out in full length, rather than in abbreviated tweet speak.

The collection of twisdoms is organized by topic. Topics are organized by month, according to the seasonal popularity of each topic. For example, advice concerning scholarships is provided in September, the CSS/Financial Aid PROFILE form in October, repaying student loans in November, the Free Application for Federal Student Aid (FAFSA) in January, increasing aid eligibility in February, evaluating award letters in March, education tax benefits in April, saving for college in May and borrowing student loans in June.

What is an Effective Twisdom?

Ideally, a twisdom should be effective in influencing consumer behavior. Effective twisdoms often demonstrate several of the following characteristics.

Simple

- Effective twisdoms are easy to learn.
- Effective twisdoms are memorable, making it easy for consumers to remember them.
- Effective twisdoms may involve alliteration, consonance, assonance or rhyming.
- Effective twisdoms are specific, not vague.
- Effective twisdoms are easy to apply.
- Effective twisdoms communicate a single, well-defined concept.
- Effective twisdoms are simple in all aspects.
- Effective twisdoms are short and concise, fitting into just a few sentences, even if they don't fit into Twitter's 140-character limit.

Actionable

- Effective twisdoms can be personalized to the consumer's specific circumstances.
- Effective twisdoms are designed to cause consumers to take a specific action.

- Effective twisdoms may involve simple comparisons, but do not require complicated calculations.
- Effective twisdoms are not necessarily optimal or perfect. Rather, they are "good enough" approximations that trade accuracy and precision for ease of use.
- Effective twisdoms provide insights that sound plausible without having to think through the details first.

Improve Decision-Making

- Effective twisdoms help the consumer make decisions and reach conclusions.
- Effective twisdoms help people make decisions quickly and efficiently with minimal information.

A good sign of an effective twisdom is when others adopt the twisdom as their own, even claiming to have invented it themselves. When a twisdom becomes part of the "general knowledge," it helps the twisdom spread among consumers. The first step in having an impact often involves giving up ownership of an idea.

Top Twenty Twisdoms

Savings and Scholarships

1) It is cheaper to save than to borrow.
2) Every dollar you save or win is about a dollar less you'll have to borrow.
3) Save a fifth of your income for the last fifth of your life.
4) College costs triple in the 17 years from birth to college enrollment.
5) You can't get any aid if you don't apply.
6) If you have to pay money to get money, it is probably a scam.

FAFSA

7) File the FAFSA as soon as possible after January 1. Do not wait for tax returns to be completed or for college admissions decisions.
8) Students who file the FAFSA in January, February and March receive more than double the grants, on average, of students who file the FAFSA later in the financial aid application cycle.

Loans (Borrowing)

9) Live like a student while you are in school, so you don't have to live like a student after you graduate.
10) Every dollar you borrow will cost about two dollars by the time you repay the debt.

11) Education debt may be good debt because it is an investment in the student's future, but too much of a good thing can hurt you.
12) Budget before you borrow.
13) Keep debt in sync with income. Total student loan debt at graduation should be less than the borrower's annual starting salary, and, ideally, a lot less.
14) Borrow federal first, as federal student loans are cheaper, more available and have better repayment terms than private student loans.
15) A cosigner is a co-borrower, equally obligated to repay the debt. Cosigning a student loan may be hazardous to your wealth.

Student Employment

16) Students who work 40 or more hours a week during the academic year are half as likely to graduate as students who work 12 hours or less a week.

Loans (Repayment)

17) Monthly loan payments on a 10-year repayment term are approximately 1% of the amount borrowed.
18) Choose the repayment plan with the highest monthly payment you can afford, to save the most money over the life of the loan.
19) Accelerate repayment of the loan with the highest interest rate first to save the most money by reducing the average interest rate on the borrower's loans.

20) Students who drop out of college are four times more likely to default on their student loans than students who graduate from college.

September

September is National College Savings Month. See also May 29 (5/29), which is National College Savings Day.

The Siemens Competition in Math, Science and Technology has a scholarship deadline in September. Visit siemenscompetition.discoveryeducation.com for more information.

Applying for College Admissions

A match school is a college where the student's test scores are within the normal range admitted by the college (25th to 75th percentile).

A reach school is a college where the student's test scores are below the normal range admitted by the college (< 25th percentile).

A safety school is a college where the student's test scores are above the normal range admitted by the college (> 75th percentile).

A financial aid safety school is a college where the student could afford to enroll even if he or she does not get any financial aid.

Need-blind colleges do not necessarily meet the full demonstrated need of all admitted students, leading to an "admit-deny" situation.

Need-blind colleges may become need-sensitive for transfer students, international students and wait-listed students.

Chances of Winning a Scholarship

Parents have a tendency to *overestimate* their child's eligibility for merit-based aid and to *underestimate* their child's eligibility for need-based financial aid.

Only about 1 in 8 students in Bachelor's degree programs have won private scholarships, on average about $4,000 per year.

Less than 1% of students in Bachelor's degree programs win a completely free ride.

Private scholarships are part of the plan for paying for college, but not the entire plan.

How to Search for College Scholarships

Every dollar you win in scholarships is about a dollar less you'll have to borrow.

Scholarships are part of the plan for paying for college, but not the entire plan.

Students of all ages can apply for scholarships. You don't need to be a high school senior to win scholarships.

About half of all scholarships have deadlines in the fall, so don't wait until the spring to start searching for scholarships.

Start searching for scholarships ASAP. Many scholarships are available to students in younger grades, not just during the senior year in high school. See www.edvisors.com/age13 for a list.

Search for scholarships at free scholarship search sites, such as StudentScholarshipSearch.com and CollegeBoard.org.

When using a scholarship matching service, answer all the optional questions. Students who answer the optional questions tend to match about twice as many scholarships as students who answer only the required questions.

The optional questions in a scholarship matching service trigger the inclusion of specific scholarships in the search results.

How to Win College Scholarships

Winning scholarships involves a bit of luck, not just skill. Increase your chances of winning a scholarship by applying to every scholarship for which you are eligible.

You can't win a scholarship if you don't apply.

Applying for scholarships gets easier after your first half-dozen applications, since you'll be able to reuse your essays, tailoring them to each new application.

Maintain a professional online appearance, just as you would want to present a professional appearance in a face-to-face interview. Google your name. Remove inappropriate tweets and Facebook posts.

Use a professional email address, such as firstname.lastname@gmail.com.

When writing essays, try recording yourself as you answer the question out loud. Then, transcribe the recording and add structure by organizing and outlining your thoughts.

Most people write or type at about 30-60 words per minute and speak at about 200 words per minute, so the act of writing interferes with the flow of thought.

Small scholarships with a top prize of less than $1,000 and essay contests are usually less competitive and easier to win and help you win bigger scholarships.

Take the PSAT/NMSQT in the fall of the junior year in high school. This is the qualifying test for the National Merit Scholarship, a major scholarship program.

Scholarship Scams and Other Pitfalls

Scholarship programs are about giving away money, not getting money. Do not apply to a scholarship that charges any kind of an application fee.

If you have to pay money to get money, it is probably a scam.

Never invest more than a postage stamp to get information about scholarships or to apply for a scholarship.

Nobody can guarantee that you'll win a scholarship.

Do not give out bank account numbers, credit card numbers or Social Security Numbers when applying for a scholarship.

Beware of the unclaimed aid myth. The only scholarships that ever go unclaimed can't be claimed, such as scholarships with very restrictive selection criteria.

October

The CSS/Financial Aid PROFILE form becomes available starting October 1.

High school juniors take the PSAT/NMSQT in October to enter the National Merit Scholarship Program.

The Coca-Cola Scholars Program Scholarship (www.coca-colascholarsfoundation.org) has an October scholarship deadline.

Taxpayers who received an automatic 6-month filing extension must file their federal income tax returns by October 15.

CSS/Financial Aid PROFILE Form

The CSS/Financial Aid PROFILE Form is used by about 225 colleges for awarding their own financial aid funds and more than 100 scholarship competitions.

October 1 is the first day an applicant can file the CSS/Financial Aid PROFILE form.

If your college or scholarship competition requires the CSS/Financial Aid PROFILE, file it on or after October 1.

Differences between the FAFSA and CSS/Financial Aid PROFILE

The FAFSA divides the parent contribution portion of the EFC by number of children in college in the next academic year. The CSS/Financial Aid PROFILE uses a smaller reduction in the parent contribution.

The FAFSA ignores assets for low-income families; the CSS/Financial Aid PROFILE does not.

The FAFSA looks at one year of income; the CSS/Financial Aid PROFILE looks at three years of income data.

The FAFSA season starts January 1; the CSS/Financial Aid PROFILE season begins on October 1.

The CSS/Financial Aid PROFILE counts certain assets that are ignored on the FAFSA: family home, small businesses, paper losses, non-custodial parent assets, sibling assets.

The CSS/Financial Aid PROFILE has more questions than the FAFSA, designed to prevent wealthy students from looking poor.

The CSS/Financial Aid PROFILE has regional cost of living adjustments, as well as allowances for college savings and emergencies.

The CSS/Financial Aid PROFILE requires a minimum student contribution or summer work expectation.

November

November is National Scholarship Month.

Student loan repayment begins in November for May/June college graduates, after the end of the 6-month grace period.

Early admission applications have earlier deadlines than the regular college admission process, typically November 1 instead of January 1.

The Jif Most Creative Sandwich Contest (www.jif.com/Promotions/Most-Creative-Peanut-Butter/), Jack Kent Cooke Foundation scholarships (www.jkcf.org/scholarship-programs/), Prudential Spirit of Community Awards (spirit.prudential.com) and Intel Science Talent Search (https://student.societyforscience.org/intel-sts) have scholarship deadlines in November.

Dealing with Financial Difficulty

Borrowers who graduate with too much student loan debt often have problems with their credit cards and other forms of consumer credit, too.

Increasing awareness of spending patterns is the first step toward exercising financial restraint.

Save on rent by moving to a cheaper apartment, getting a roommate or moving back into your parent's house.

Sell your car and either replace it with a bicycle or a cheap used car or use public transportation.

Sell excess belongings on eBay or Craigslist to pay down your student loan debt. If you haven't used an item in more than a year, you probably don't need it.

Adopt an austere lifestyle. Do not eat out or participate in paid entertainment unless someone else is paying.

Wait at least a week before buying anything expensive to make sure you really need it.

Use cash instead of credit. Spending $500 with a credit card feels the same as spending $5, making it more difficult to exercise restraint. Using cash makes it feel like you are spending money, especially if you don't carry big bills. If you set aside a fixed amount of cash to spend each month, the spending will stop when you run out of money.

Get a second job in the evenings and weekends. Not only will this earn extra money to pay down debt, but you'll also have less time to spend money.

Create a Descriptive Budget

Start with a descriptive budget, not a prescriptive budget. Track all spending for a month. Get receipts for every purchase and record them every evening in a spreadsheet or personal finance program like Mint.com or Quicken.

Classify the expenses into broad categories like food, clothing, housing, medical care, insurance, taxes, loan payments, transportation, dining and entertainment.

Also, label expenses as mandatory (need) or discretionary (want). A mandatory expense is one where you would die or go to jail if you didn't spend the money.

Cell phones and cable/satellite TV are luxuries, not necessities. (Cell phone service is not needed to make emergency calls. All modern cell phones will dial 911 for emergencies even without subscribing to a carrier's service plan.)

Managing Student Loan Repayment

To avoid forgetting about a loan, make a list of all your loans, including lender contact information, loan id number, interest rates, loan balance, monthly payment and repayment plan.

Add a note to your calendar two weeks before the first payment is due on each loan. The payment is due even if you don't receive a coupon book or statement from the lender.

Visit www.edvisors.com/repay-student-loans/ for tips about repaying student loans and loan forgiveness.

Saving Money While Repaying Student Loans

Borrowers who sign up for auto-debit with electronic billing, where monthly loan payments are automatically transferred from the borrower's bank account, may qualify for a 0.25% or 0.50% interest rate reduction.

The student loan interest deduction provides an above-the-line exclusion from income for up to $2,500 in interest on federal and private student loans each year on the borrower's federal income tax return. This deduction can be claimed even if the taxpayer does not itemize.

Public service loan forgiveness cancels the remaining debt after the borrower has made 120 on-time monthly payments (10 years of payments) on his/her federal student loans in the Direct Loan program while working full-time in a public service job. The monthly loan payments must have been made under the standard repayment, income-contingent repayment, income-based repayment or pay-as-you-earn repayment plans.

Loan payments are applied first to late fees and collection charges, next to accrued but unpaid interest and last to the principal balance of the loan. The difference between different repayment plans is manifested in the amount applied to the principal balance of the loan. Changing the repayment term of a loan from 10 years to 20 years, but continuing to make the monthly payments from the 10-year repayment term, is the same as having a 10-year repayment term.

Accelerating Loan Repayment

There are no prepayment penalties on federal and private student loans, so nothing stops you from making extra payments on your loans.

A prepayment penalty is a fee charged if a borrower makes a full or partial prepayment on the debt, in addition to the regularly scheduled loan payments.

Prepaying a loan is like earning a tax-free return on investment at the loan's interest rate, since it avoids paying interest at that rate on the amount prepaid.

Make extra payments to reduce the principal balance on the loan with the highest interest rate first to save the most money.

Pay off high-interest debt, such as credit card debt, first. Any consumer indebtedness with double-digit interest rates should be paid off before considering potential investments.

Avoid the snowball effect, which tries to pay off the smallest loans first. Proponents say it gives the borrower a psychological boost when a loan is paid off. But, in the long term, this will cost more than paying off the highest-rate loans first.

Accelerating repayment of the loan with the highest interest rate, as opposed to the smallest loan, reduces the average interest rate on the borrower's loans.

Don't consolidate student loans when accelerating repayment. A consolidation loan replaces the old loans with a single loan, preventing the borrower from targeting a specific loan for quicker repayment.

Invest extra money in the opportunity with the highest after-tax return on investment.

Choosing a Repayment Plan

Choose the repayment plan with the highest monthly payment you can afford, to save the most money over the life of the loan.

Minimize the repayment term to reduce the cost of the loan.

Stretching out the repayment term reduces the monthly loan payment, but also increases the total interest paid over the life of the loan.

Monthly loan payments on a 10-year repayment term are approximately 1% of the amount borrowed.

Extended repayment reduces the monthly payment by increasing the repayment term of the loan to 15, 20, 25 or more years. But, this also increases the total interest paid over the life of the loan.

Borrowers who use extended repayment or income-based repayment may have to postpone certain life-cycle events, such as getting married, buying a home and saving for retirement. For example, they may still be repaying their own student loans when their children enroll in college. This means they will be less likely to save and less willing to borrow for their children's college education, because they will still be up to their eyebrows in debt.

Negative amortization occurs when the loan payments are less than the new interest that accrues.

Negative amortization can be very harmful to the affordability of a loan, since unpaid interest is added to the loan balance, increasing the amount of debt. About half of borrowers in income-contingent repayment (ICR), income-based repayment (IBR) and pay-as-you-earn repayment (PAYER) are negatively amortized.

Instead of a forbearance (a temporary suspension of all loan payments), which is negatively amortized, consider a partial forbearance, where monthly payments equal at least the new interest that accrues.

Consolidation Loans

Beware of companies charging fees to consolidate federal education loans. When you deal directly with the federal government, there are no fees to consolidate federal education loans.

Visit www.StudentLoans.gov to consolidate federal loans and change repayment plans.

A consolidation loan replaces several loans with a single loan.

A consolidation loan refinances existing loans by making a new loan that pays off the old loans.

The interest rate on a federal consolidation loan is based on the weighted average of the interest rates on the old loans, rounded up to the nearest 1/8th of a point.

Consolidation doesn't always save the borrower money. If the interest rates on the borrower's student loans differ by several percentage points, targeting the loan with the highest interest rate for quicker repayment may save more money than refinancing the loans.

Federal consolidation loans do not save the borrower money, as the interest rates on federal education loans are already fixed.

Private consolidation loans may save the borrower money, if the borrower's credit scores have improved significantly since the loans were borrowed. This usually requires the borrower to make several years of on-time payments, never be late with a payment, not even a day late, on all the borrower's debts, not just the student loans. The private consolidation loan is a new loan with a new interest rate based on the borrower's current credit scores.

Visit www.studentloanconsolidator.com to refinance private student loans.

Mortgages and Student Loans

Borrowers who are paying all their debts on-time but who are having trouble qualifying for a mortgage should consider switching to an extended repayment plan or income-based repayment. These repayment plans reduce the monthly payment. Mortgage lenders base their credit underwriting decisions on the percentage of gross monthly income that is used to repay debts, not the total amount owed.

Mortgage lenders base credit underwriting decisions on the debt-service-to-income ratio, which is the percentage of gross monthly income that is required to repay all of the borrower's debt. They do not consider the debt-to-income ratio, which is the ratio of total debt to annual income. So, one way a student loan borrower can increase the likelihood of qualifying for a mortgage is to choose a student loan repayment plan that yields a lower monthly payment, such as extended repayment or income-based repayment.

Cosigners who are unable to refinance a mortgage because they have too much debt should ask the primary borrower of the private student loan to seek a cosigner release or private consolidation to remove the loans from the cosigner's credit history.

Student Loan Default

Almost two-thirds of students who default on their student loans dropped out of college.

Students who drop out of college are four times more likely to default on their student loans than students who graduate from college.

Students who graduate with total student loan debt that is more than double their annual income are at very high risk of defaulting on the debt.

The monthly payments under income-based repayment are usually less than the monthly payments under wage garnishment, so there is no financial benefit to defaulting on federal student loans.

The federal government has very strong powers to compel repayment on defaulted federal education loans. The federal government can garnish up to 15% of wages and offset up to 15% of Social Security disability and retirement benefit payments. The federal government can also seize federal and state income tax refunds and state lottery winnings to repay defaulted federal education loans. Up to 20% of payments on a defaulted federal student loan will be deducted to pay for collection charges, before the remainder is applied to the interest and principal balance of the loan. This slows the repayment trajectory significantly. Borrowers who are in default on a federal education loan are ineligible for FHA and VA mortgages. They cannot enlist in the U.S. Armed Forces and the federal government can block renewal of a professional license. Borrowers who are in default will have difficulty getting a credit card, auto loan or mortgage. Landlords who check the borrower's credit may be unwilling to rent an apartment to a defaulted borrower. Some employers will check the credit history of a prospective employee before deciding whether to hire him or her.

Bankruptcy and Student Loans

Student loans are almost impossible to discharge in bankruptcy. You are more likely to get cancer or die in a car crash than to have your student loans discharged in bankruptcy.

Bankruptcy court judges require a "certainty of hopelessness" before they will discharge student loans.

Struggling to Repay Student Loans

When borrowers report that the balance on their loan has doubled, it almost always involves an extended period of non-payment.

Avoid extended periods of nonpayment, because they significantly increase the amount of debt.

Interest continues to accumulate during a deferment or forbearance. If the interest is not paid as it accrues, it will be capitalized (added to the loan balance), digging you into a deeper hole.

Unemployed borrowers can volunteer with AmeriCorps to earn education awards that can be used to pay down student loan debt.

Students who graduate with excessive debt tend to delay life-cycle events, such as buying a car, getting married, having children, buying a home and saving for retirement.

Students who graduate with excessive debt or who default on their student loans are more likely to be depressed.

Borrowing excessive student loans can be like having a mortgage without owning a home.

If a borrower is struggling to repay his or her student loans, the last thing he or she needs is to pile on more debt through a home mortgage, credit cards, additional student loans or other consumer debt.

If total student loan debt exceeds annual income, the borrower will struggle to repay the debt and will need alternate repayment plans, like extended repayment or income-based repayment, to afford the monthly loan payments.

If Social Security disability and retirement benefits are being offset to repay federal student loan debt, consider rehabilitating the loans and switching into income-based repayment. This may reduce the monthly payments.

Retiring with Student Loan Debt

Try to pay off all debts by the time you retire, as there is usually no new income in retirement, just assets.

If you are retiring with debt and cannot afford to pay off the debt, consider using extended repayment or income-based repayment to reduce the monthly payments by stretching out the term of the loan. Federal education loans, including the Federal Parent PLUS loan, are cancelled when the borrower dies and are not charged against the borrower's estate.

December

The AXA Achievement Scholarships (www.axa-achievement.com) and the Elks Most Valuable Student Competition (www.elks.org/enf/scholars/) have scholarship deadlines in December.

College Affordability

The failure of grants to keep pace with increases in college costs causes declines in college affordability.

Student loan debt continues to grow faster than income, driven by a failure of federal and state government grants to keep pace with increases in college costs.

Federal and state governments have been cutting their support of higher education on a per-student, constant dollar basis for decades.

The burden of paying for college has shifted from federal and state government to families. Since family income is flat, families must either increase debt or shift enrollment to lower-cost colleges.

Declines in college affordability force students to graduate with thousands of dollars of additional debt or to shift their enrollment to lower-cost colleges.

Student loans are the only form of financial aid that demonstrates any degree of elasticity.

The higher a college's net price, the higher the average education debt at graduation.

Typically, the least expensive college is an in-state public college. Colleges with generous "no loans" financial aid policies that replace loans with grants in the financial aid package are also among the least expensive.

The shift in enrollment from 4-year colleges to 2-year colleges causes a decline in Bachelor's degree attainment.

Of students who intend to obtain a Bachelor's degree, only 1/5 of those who start at a 2-year college graduate with a Bachelor's degree within 6 years, compared with 2/3 of students who start at a 4-year college.

Low-income students are more likely to enroll in 2-year colleges and less likely to enroll in and graduate from 4-year colleges than high-income students.

Low- and moderate-income students are increasingly being priced out of a college education.

The main problem is the *amount* of debt, not the *cost* of debt.

Sticker shock refers to the anxiety and dismay students and parents feel when they learn about the total cost of attendance of the student's dream college or university.

An admit-deny situation occurs when a college grants admission to a student but fails to award the student the financial aid he or she needs to be able to afford to enroll at the college.

January

The Free Application for Federal Student Aid (FAFSA) becomes available starting January 1.

The Dell Scholars Program (www.dellscholars.org), Gates Millennium Scholars Program (www.gmsp.org), Ron Brown Scholars Program (www.ronbrown.org) and Burger King Scholars Program (www.bkmclamorefoundation.org) have scholarship deadlines in January.

Free Application for Federal Student Aid (FAFSA)

The FAFSA stands for the Free Application for Federal Student Aid.

The FAFSA is used to apply for student aid from the federal government, state government and most colleges and universities.

The FAFSA is a prerequisite for obtaining low-cost federal education loans, not just government grants and student employment.

File the FAFSA as soon as possible on or after January 1.

Do not wait until your federal income tax returns have been filed or the student has been admitted to a college to file the FAFSA.

Students who file the FAFSA in January, February and March receive more than double the grants, on average, of students who file the FAFSA later.

The FAFSA is used to apply for state and college aid, not just federal aid.

Some states and colleges have very early deadlines or award aid on first-come, first-served basis.

Nine states award aid on a first-come, first-served basis: IL, KY, NC, SC, TN, TX, VT, WA and DC.

Three states have February deadlines and eleven states have March deadlines for the FAFSA.

Free FAFSA Help

The best-selling book, *Filing the FAFSA*, is available for free download in PDF format at www.edvisors.com/fafsa-book

Federal Student Aid Information Center runs a toll-free hotline on FAFSA at 1-800-4-FED-AID (1-800-433-3243).

College Goal Sunday runs free FAFSA completion workshops in January-March. Visit www.collegegoalsundayusa.org.

Number of Schools on the FAFSA

FAFSA on the Web allows applicants to list up to 10 schools at a time.

To list more than 10 colleges on the FAFSA: list 10, wait until the Student Aid Report (SAR) arrives, then delete the original colleges to add new ones.

When the SAR arrives, it is a sign that the schools listed on the FAFSA have received the student's information.

To change colleges listed on the FAFSA, login at fafsa.ed.gov, select "Make FAFSA Corrections" then go to "School Selection" page.

Colleges can also add themselves to your FAFSA if you give them the Data Release Number (DRN) listed on your Student Aid Report (SAR).

Order of Schools on the FAFSA

All colleges listed on the FAFSA can see the order in which colleges are listed on the FAFSA

The order of colleges on the FAFSA may tell colleges about a student's college preferences.

If a college is listed first on a student's FAFSA and the student is admitted, the student will enroll at that college more than half the time.

If a college is listed second on a student's FAFSA and the student is admitted, the student will enroll at that college more than a quarter of the time.

If a college is listed third on a student's FAFSA and the student is admitted, the student will enroll at that college more than a tenth of the time.

If first choice college is a reach, perhaps list it second or third on the FAFSA, so the second choice school can be listed first.

If the student is applying for state aid, list a state school first on the FAFSA, such as one in the student's state of legal residence.

Always Apply for Financial Aid

You can't get aid if you don't apply.

Unfortunately, many students don't file the FAFSA. Two million students would have got a Federal Pell Grant, if only they had filed the FAFSA.

Of the students who didn't file a FAFSA, 1.3 million would have got a full Federal Pell Grant.

Families should file the FAFSA every year, even if they got nothing other than loans last year.

FAFSA Errors

Male students age 18-26 should remember to register with Selective Service, as failing to register may affect the student's eligibility for federal, state and institutional aid.

Do not report qualified retirement plans or the net worth of the family home in the answer to the question about investments on the FAFSA. They are not considered reportable assets on the FAFSA.

Don't file the wrong year's FAFSA. From January to June there are two versions of the FAFSA, one for the current academic year and one for the upcoming academic year. About 90% of applicants should be filing the latter, but figuring out which form to file can be confusing. Always check the college's web site to learn about key application deadlines and required forms.

Double-check all numbers on the FAFSA. Beware of transposing adjacent digits or writing a number in the wrong field.

FAFSA Error: digit transpositions and typos in numbers and dollar amounts.

FAFSA Error: Failing to file the FAFSA; thereby, missing out on student aid.

FAFSA Error: Filing the wrong year's FAFSA

FAFSA Error: Missing deadlines. File the FAFSA ASAP on or after January 1. Some states and schools have very early FAFSA deadlines or award aid on a first-come, first-served basis.

FAFSA Error: Not counting stepchildren in the family household size. If the stepparent provides half support, count the stepchildren even if they live elsewhere.

FAFSA Error: Not including stepparent's income and assets

FAFSA Error: Not notifying financial aid administrator of special circumstances

FAFSA Error: Problems with reported marital status

FAFSA Error: Providing wrong parent's financial information.

FAFSA Error: Social Security Numbers, names and dates of birth do not match for each person listed on the FAFSA.

Use whole dollar amounts on the FAFSA and other financial aid application forms. Do not use cents, as this can cause your income, assets and taxes to be overstated.

When applying for financial aid, use your legal name as it appears on your Social Security card. Do not use your nickname, maiden name or middle name, as this will cause a database mismatch reject.

The terms "you" and "your" on the FAFSA refer to the student applicant, not the parent.

Dependency Status

All students are dependent unless they satisfy the criteria for independent student status.

A dependent student must include parental information on financial aid application forms. Independent students do not report parental information on their financial aid application forms.

If you will be age 24 or older by December 31 of the academic year for which you are seeking financial aid, you are independent.

If you are currently married, you are independent.

If you are on active duty with the U.S. Armed Forces for purposes other than training, or a veteran, you are independent.

If you have children who will receive more than half support from you during the academic year, you are independent.

If you have a dependent (not child/spouse) who lives with and receives more than half of his/her support from you now and through end of academic year for which you are seeking financial aid, you are independent.

If you are or were a court-ordered emancipated minor *prior* to reaching the age of majority, you are independent.

Note that legal emancipation must be court-ordered, and prior to reaching age of majority. End of child support does not count.

If you are or were determined to be an unaccompanied youth who was homeless or who were self-supporting and at risk of being homeless, you are independent.

If you are or were in a court-ordered legal guardianship (attorney not enough) prior to reaching the age of majority, you are independent.

If you were, at any time since turning age 13, an orphan, in foster care, or a dependent or ward of the court, you are independent.

If you will be a graduate or professional student at the start of the academic year for which you are seeking financial aid, you are independent.

Unaccompanied and homeless or self-supporting and at risk of homelessness, may be independent.

If the student has an extreme or unusual situation (physical/sexual/mental abuse, both parents incarcerated/institutionalized, abandonment), ask the college for a dependency override.

If you are granted a dependency override by a college financial aid administrator because of unusual circumstances, you are independent.

Who is a Parent on the FAFSA

Report marital status as of the date the FAFSA is filed. Do not anticipate a future change in marital status. The data on the FAFSA should be accurate as of the date the FAFSA is filed.

If a student's parents are married or living together, information from both parents must be reported on the FAFSA.

If the student's parents are unmarried (divorced, never-married) but living together, they are treated as though they are married on the FAFSA.

When a student's parents are divorced or separated or never married, and do not live together, only one parent is responsible for completing the FAFSA. This is the "custodial" parent.

The “custodial” parent is the one with whom the student lived the most during the 12 months before filing the FAFSA.

If a dependent student's parents are divorced or separated and do not live together, only the custodial parent is responsible for filing the FAFSA.

Informal separation (not just legal separation) counts as a separation on the FAFSA, but a couple can't cohabit (live together) with an informal separation.

If the student lived equally with both parents in the last 12 months, the custodial parent is the parent who provided more financial support to the student.

If the student’s custodial parent has remarried, the stepparent’s information must be reported, regardless of any prenuptial agreements. Also, the family should count stepchildren from previous marriages in the household size if the student’s stepparent or custodial parent provides more than half of their support, even if they don’t live with the student’s stepparent and custodial parent. If these children are enrolled in college, they may be able to be counted in the number in college as well, which can lead to a reduction in the expected family contribution and an increase in eligibility for need-based financial aid.

Impact of Income on Eligibility for Need-Based Aid

Every $10,000 in *parent* income will reduce eligibility for need-based financial aid by about $3,000. Every $10,000 in *student* income will reduce eligibility for need-based financial aid by as much as $5,000.

Half of dependent student income above about $6,000, including untaxed income, will reduce eligibility for need-based financial aid.

Simplified Needs Test and Auto-Zero EFC

If parent adjusted gross income (AGI) is less than $24,000 and certain other conditions are satisfied, the student's FAFSA may qualify for the Automatic Zero EFC (Expected Family Contribution). This test causes the student's expected family contribution (EFC) to be set at zero, making the student eligible for the maximum Federal Pell Grant. Consider reducing Adjusted Gross Income (AGI) below $24,000 to qualify for Auto-Zero EFC

If parent adjusted gross income (AGI) is less than $50,000 and certain other conditions are satisfied, the student's FAFSA may qualify for the Simplified Needs Test. The Simplified Needs Test causes all assets to be ignored on the FAFSA. Consider reducing income below $50,000 to qualify for the Simplified Needs Test.

Impact of Assets on Eligibility for Need-Based Aid

Net worth is the difference between the market value of an asset and any outstanding debts secured by the asset.

Parent assets are sheltered by an asset protection allowance, typically $30,000 to $50,000, based on the age of the older parent living with the student.

Parent assets on the FAFSA reduce aid eligibility by as much as 5.64% of the net worth of the asset.

Student assets are assessed more heavily than parent assets. Eligibility for need-based financial aid is reduced by 20% of student assets versus at most 5.64% of the net worth of the parent assets.

Reporting 529 Plans on the FAFSA

If a 529 college savings plan is owned by a dependent student or the student's parent, it is reported as a parent asset on the FAFSA.

If a 529 college savings plan is reported as an asset on the FAFSA, distributions are not reported as income.

Number of Children in College

The number of children enrolled in college at the same time can have a big impact on each child's eligibility for need-based financial aid.

The parent contribution portion of the expected family contribution is divided by the number of children in college.

The children do not have to live with the parent; they just have to get 1/2 of their support from the parent.

Parents can increase the number of children in college at the same time by spacing the children closer together or by having one child skip a grade or take a gap year to increase the overlap.

February

The IRS Data Retrieval Tool can be used starting the first Sunday in February.

February is Financial Aid Awareness Month.

The Buick Achievers Scholarship Program (www.buickachievers.com) and Davidson Fellows Scholarships (www.davidsongifted.org) have scholarship deadlines in February.

Demonstrated Financial Need

Need-based financial aid is based on demonstrated financial need, which is the difference between college costs and the expected family contribution (EFC). Demonstrated financial need increases with increases in college costs and decreases in the EFC.

The expected family contribution (EFC) is a measure of the family's financial strength that is used to determine the student's eligibility for student financial aid.

Middle- and high-income students who don't qualify for aid at a public college might qualify for aid at a higher-cost private non-profit college.

Increase Eligibility for Aid: General Tips

Test financial aid strategies before using them.

Increase Eligibility for Aid: Income

The base year for financial aid application forms begins January 1 of the junior year in high school. Avoid artificially increasing income through capital gains or retirement plan distributions during the base year and each subsequent year.

Methods of reducing income include deferring bonuses and retirement plan distributions to a subsequent year, minimizing capital gains or offsetting capital gains with losses, and increasing above-the-line exclusions from income (such as contributions to a 401(k) retirement plan).

Avoid artificial increases in income, such as capital gains, retirement plan distributions, employment bonuses and exercising stock options during the base year.

Realize capital gains prior to January 1 of the student's junior year in high school, so that the artificial increase in income does not affect eligibility for need-based financial aid.

Try to minimize capital gains or offset gains with losses. Capital gains are treated like income.

Offset capital gains with losses to reduce impact on aid eligibility.

Untaxed income to the student reduces aid eligibility by as much as half the distribution amount, just like taxable income.

If parent income is close to $24,000 or $50,000, look into the auto-zero EFC and simplified needs test.

If parents are divorced or separated, have the children live with the parent with the lower income (including stepparent income).

Increase Eligibility for Aid: Assets

Money in qualified retirement plans is ignored on the FAFSA, as are certain small family businesses and the family home.

Report assets as of the date the FAFSA is filed, not the end of the last calendar year. If you will be making a last-minute change in your assets, try to make the change early enough so that it will appear on the last monthly statement before you file the FAFSA. Always print out a snapshot of your account's balance from the financial institution's web site on the day the FAFSA is submitted. Retain a copy of these balance statements in case a college requests this information.

Spend down student assets to zero before spending any of the parent assets. Student assets can be used to pay for SAT/ACT test prep, tutoring, a computer for school, dormitory furnishings and/or a car to commute to college as well as college tuition and fees and other college costs. Since assets are reported as of the date the FAFSA is filed, spending down assets should occur before filing the FAFSA in the student's high school senior year, not afterward.

Accelerate necessary expenses to reduce assets before filing the FAFSA.

Paying down unsecured consumer debt, such as credit cards and auto loans, and paying down the mortgage on the family's principal place of residence may increase eligibility for need based financial aid.

Pay down debt to shelter money from the financial aid formula and to save on interest. But, always keep 3-6 month's salary in an emergency fund.

Avoid trust funds and home equity loans because of their impact on financial aid eligibility. Trust funds almost always backfire.

Save money in the parent's name, not the child's, to qualify for more aid. Main exception: custodial 529 plans are treated as parent assets.

To qualify for the small business exclusion on the FAFSA, the business must have less than 100 full-time or full-time equivalent employees.

To qualify for the small business exclusion on the FAFSA, the family must own more than half the business: 51%, not 50%.

Increase Eligibility for Aid: 529 College Savings Plans

If a 529 college savings plan is reported as an asset on the FAFSA, qualified distributions are ignored.

If a 529 college savings plan is not reported as an asset on the FAFSA, distributions are reported as untaxed income to the student.

If a 529 college savings plan is owned by a dependent student or the dependent student's custodial parent, it is reported as a parent asset on the FAFSA.

If a 529 college savings plan is owned by an independent student, it is reported as a student asset on the FAFSA.

If a 529 college savings plan is owned by a grandparent, non-custodial parent, aunt, uncle, etc., it is not reported as an asset on the FAFSA.

If you save in the parent's name or in a student- or parent-owned 529 college savings plan, the penalty for saving is minimal. Every $10,000 in the *parent's* name reduces aid eligibility by $564. This leaves the family with $9,436 to pay for college costs, giving them more options than families who did not save for college.

On the FAFSA, qualified distributions from non-reportable assets, such as grandparent-owned 529 college savings plans and Roth IRAs, count as untaxed income to the beneficiary. This reduces student eligibility for need-based aid by as much as half of the distribution amount.

Beware of the impact of distributions from grandparent-owned 529 plans. Change the account owner or wait until student's senior year in college to take distributions (unless the student is planning to attend graduate/professional school in the next academic year).

Increase Eligibility for Aid: Number in College

Increase number of children in college at the same time. Parent contribution is divided by number of children in college.

Increasing number of children in college at the same time from 1 to 2 is like dividing parent income in half.

Increase Eligibility for Aid: Dependency Status

Dependency status can affect eligibility for need-based financial aid.

Increase Eligibility for Aid: Timing of Aid

Carve out $4,000 in tuition and textbook costs to be paid with cash, not 529 plan distributions, to qualify for American Opportunity Tax Credit.

The number of Federal Pell Grants a student is eligible to receive is subject to a lifetime limit that is the equivalent of 6 academic years. Students who expect to receive a small Federal Pell Grant may wish to forgo the grant one year in order to preserve eligibility for a larger grant in a subsequent year.

Packaging Philosophy

The financial aid package combines different types of aid from many sources - school, state, federal government, private sources – to help the student pay for college.

Each college has a different "packaging philosophy" which specifies how it awards financial aid to financially needy students.

Some schools leave a gap (unmet need), sometimes called a minimum student contribution or summer work expectations. Unmet need is the difference between the student's demonstrated financial need and the student's financial aid package.

Some colleges have a self-help level which is met with student loans and student employment before awarding any grants.

Others have "no loans" financial aid policies, substituting grants for loans in the financial aid package.

Verification

About one-third of FAFSAs filed each year are selected for verification, where the applicant must supply documentation for data elements on the FAFSA.

The focus of verification is on reducing errors on the FAFSA, especially errors that affect eligibility for the Federal Pell Grant.

The U.S. Department of Education uses a risk-based model to select FAFSAs for verification.

Low-income students are more likely to be selected for verification than high-income students.

IRS Data Retrieval Tool

The IRS Data Retrieval Tool transfers income and tax information from your federal income tax return to the FAFSA.

The IRS Data Retrieval Tool can be used starting the first Sunday in February.

Use the IRS Data Retrieval Tool to update the FAFSA a few weeks after you have filed your federal income tax returns.

Any data elements transferred to the FAFSA using the IRS Data Retrieval Tool without modification will not be subject to verification.

To reduce the chances of a FAFSA being selected for verification of income and tax information, use the IRS Data Retrieval Tool.

March

College admissions acceptances and financial aid award letters arrive in late March and early April.

The Kohl's Cares Scholarship Program (www.kohlscorporation.com/CommunityRelations/scholarship/) has a scholarship deadline in March.

Evaluate College Costs based on Net Price

Compare college costs based on the net price, the difference between total college costs and just gift aid.

Gift aid is money that does not need to be earned or repaid, such as grants, scholarships and tuition waivers.

Grants are usually awarded based on demonstrated financial need. Scholarships are usually awarded based on some form of merit, such as academic, artistic or athletic talent, or activities, such as community service.

A tuition waiver reduces or eliminates a student's tuition and fee obligation, usually in exchange for services performed by the student, such as teaching or research duties, or serving as a resident assistant in a dormitory.

Net Price = Total College Costs - Gift Aid (grants, scholarships, tuition waivers)

The net price is a discounted sticker price; the amount the family must pay from savings, income and loans to cover college costs.

The net price is the true bottom-line cost of college, the amount the student and his/her family will have to pay from savings, income and loans to cover college costs.

Don't confuse net cost with net price. *Net cost* subtracts all aid, including loans, student employment and gift aid, from college costs. *Net price* subtracts just the gift aid.

Award letters often blur the distinction between loans and grants.

A loan is a loan is a loan. Loans do not cut college costs. Loans must be repaid, usually with interest.

Loans do not cut college costs; they only postpone payment, spreading the costs out over time.

The net price can vary significantly among colleges, depending on the mix of grants and loans in the financial aid package.

The net cost tends to be close to the expected family contribution (EFC) at most colleges.

High-cost colleges may offer "merit aid" to attract full-pay students, but the net price may still be lower at in-state public colleges.

A net price calculator is an online tool that provides a personalized estimate of what it will cost to attend a specific undergraduate college.

Be careful using net price calculators to compare colleges, as accuracy of calculators may vary.

Net price calculators that ask more questions tend to be more accurate.

Take a financial literacy course in high school or college to learn how to manage money and make smarter financial decisions.

Front-Loading of Grants

Front-loading is a financial aid strategy used by colleges to award more grants and scholarships to a student in his or her first year of attendance.

Ask the college if it front-loads grants (offers better grants in the first year), as that can increase net price in subsequent academic years.

About half of all colleges practice front-loading of grants, where the college provides more grants during the freshman year than during subsequent years.

Front-loading of grants reduces the net price during the freshman year, making the college look less expensive.

Scholarship Displacement

Displacement occurs when receipt of one form of financial aid, such as a private scholarship, leads to a reduction in other forms of financial aid. Some colleges reduce student loans and student employment when a student wins a private scholarship, leading to a decrease in the net price. Others reduce their own grants and/or scholarships, yielding no net financial benefit to the student.

A student is said to be over-awarded when the total need-based financial aid exceeds the student's demonstrated financial need or when the total financial aid plus the expected family contribution exceeds the college's annual cost of attendance.

If you have many private scholarships, ask college about its outside scholarship policy, because it can affect the net price.

Private scholarships can yield a lower net price. But, scholarship displacement, where the college reduces grants when the student wins a private scholarship, leaves the net price unchanged.

Colleges must reduce need-based aid when a student receives a private scholarship.

If student wins a scholarship, need decreases, so the college's outside scholarship policy specifies the type of displacement.

If the college reduces grants or scholarships when a student wins a private scholarship, the net price will remain unchanged.

If the college reduces loans or student employment when a student wins a private scholarship, the net price will decrease.

Displacement: About 80% of colleges use scholarships to reduce loans or part-time student employment opportunities, others reduce their own grants or state grants first.

If a college reduces your grants because you won a private scholarship, ask the scholarship donor about postponing the award to a subsequent year.

Negotiation / Professional Judgment

Appeal for more aid if there are unusual family financial circumstances, such as job loss, unreimbursed medical/dental expenses and other cash-flow issues beyond the family's control.

If there are unusual family financial circumstances, ask the college financial aid administrator for a professional judgment review.

If the family has unusual circumstances, such as anything that changed from last year to this year or anything that differentiates them from the typical family, appeal for more financial aid by asking the college financial aid office for a professional judgment review.

Professional judgment (PJ) is the process by which a college financial aid administrator reviews, on a case-by-case basis, documented special circumstances affecting a student's ability to pay for college.

If financial circumstances change mid-year, appeal for more aid mid-year. Contact the financial aid office ASAP.

Some colleges call PJ a special circumstances review or financial aid appeal instead of a professional judgment review.

Special circumstances: anything that changed from last year to this year or anything unusual about the family finances or cash flow.

Unusual circumstances include anything that changed from last year to this year or anything that differentiates the family from the typical family. Common examples of unusual circumstances include job loss, salary reductions, death of a wage-earner, high unreimbursed medical/dental expenses, high dependent care costs for a special needs child or elderly parent, public K-12 tuition for siblings, parents enrolled in college, legal expenses, and parents with volatile income that varies a lot from year to year. Unusual circumstances can also include one-time events – such as a bonus, Roth IRA conversion or inheritance – that are not reflective of the family's ability to pay for college during the academic year.

Financial aid appeals are driven by documentation of the special circumstances and the financial impact on the family.

When appealing for more financial aid, provide copies of documentation of unusual circumstances and the financial impact of these circumstances on the family. Documentation should be verifiable and from an independent third party.

When contacting college or university, do not use term "negotiate." Better to say "discuss." Always be polite.

If you can't afford to be polite, you are very poor indeed.

The underlying philosophy of most financial aid formulas is to assess a portion of the family's discretionary income. Discretionary income is the income that remains after subtracting allowances for mandatory expenses, such as basic living expenses and taxes.

College financial aid administrators are more likely to make adjustments when the unusual circumstances were beyond the family's control.

Colleges are not car dealerships, where bluff and bluster can get you a better deal.

April

The deadline for filing federal income tax returns is April 15. Use the IRS Data Retrieval Tool to update the FAFSA a few weeks after filing federal income tax returns.

April is National Financial Literacy Month.

Doodle 4 Google (www.google.com/doodle4google/) has a scholarship deadline in April.

Education Tax Benefits

The American Opportunity Tax Credit yields the best direct financial benefit of all the education tax benefits.

The American Opportunity Tax Credit provides a partially refundable tax credit of up to $2,500 based on amounts paid for tuition and textbooks. The tax credit is based on 100% of the first $2,000 in qualified expenses and 25% of the second $2,000 in qualified expenses each year, for up to four years of postsecondary education.

The Lifetime Learning Tax Credit is used mostly by graduate and professional students who are ineligible for the American Opportunity Tax Credit.

Claim the student loan interest deduction on your federal income tax returns. It is an above-the-line exclusion from income, so you don't need to itemize to claim it.

The Student Loan Interest Deduction provides an above-the-line exclusion from income for up to $2,500 in interest paid on federal and private student loans.

Families often overlook the education tax benefits because they are claimed in mid-April, not when the family has to pay college bills.

Cutting College Costs

Cut college costs by enrolling in an in-state public college. Even if it takes an extra year to graduate with a Bachelor's degree, you will still graduate with less debt than at most private non-profit colleges.

Look into regional exchange programs that allow students in neighboring states to qualify for reduced in-state tuition.

Before enrolling in an out-of-state public college, look into the state residency requirements. Typically, this will require living and working in the state for at least 12 consecutive months before enrollment. Registering to vote in the state and getting a state driver's license may also be necessary. But, it can help you qualify for in-state tuition, which sometimes can cut college costs in half.

Low-income students should ask about application fee waivers and admissions test fee waivers.

Graduate on time by enrolling full-time and following a clear pathway from matriculation to completion.

Students who take a "full-time" academic program of 12 credits each academic term will not graduate in four years. On-time graduation requires taking at least 15 credits each academic term.

Take an extra class each academic term and during the summer term to accelerate your progress to an academic degree.

Get college credit through Advanced Placement (AP), International Baccalaureate (IB), College-Level Examination Program (CLEP) and Proficiency Examination Program (PEP) tests.

Graduating in three years instead of four will cut college costs by about 20%.

Plan a path from matriculation to completion, taking note of how frequently certain courses are offered and their prerequisites. This will help you graduate on time.

It is important for the student to plan a path from matriculation to completion, since some classes are offered infrequently and may have prerequisites that need to be finished first.

Switching academic majors and transferring from one college to another can add a year to your academic career and will increase your total student loan debt at graduation.

Get two degrees for the same money by double majoring. But be sure you don't finish the requirements for one degree ahead of the other. Some forms of financial aid are not available to students who have already received a Bachelor's degree.

Taking a detour through a community college on your way to a Bachelor's degree may save some money, but you may also end up missing your destination. Of students who intend to obtain a Bachelor's degree, only a fifth of those who start at a 2-year college obtain a Bachelor's degree within six years. This compares with two-thirds of students who start off at a 4-year college. If the state guarantees admission to a 4-year public college for students who graduate with an Associate's degree from one of the state's community colleges, the odds of receiving a Bachelor's degree increase to about one-third.

Live like a student while you are in school, so you don't have to live like a student after you graduate.

Living expenses represent more than half of college costs at an in-state public college.

Get a roommate to split housing costs.

Living at home during college can help students graduate with less debt.

Better to live at home with your parents while you are in school than to be forced to live with them after graduation.

Students can cut costs to close the gap, by renting or buying used textbooks and reducing the number of trips home from school.

Buy used textbooks and/or sell them back to the bookstore at the end of the academic term to save about 1/4 of textbook costs.

Save money on college costs by buying used textbooks, selling textbooks back to the college bookstore at the end of the academic term, renting textbooks, buying etextbooks or by borrowing the textbooks from the college library or course instructors. Use the textbook's ISBN to search online for discounted copies. You can also save on textbook costs by sharing textbooks with classmates, your roommate or a friend.

Cut travel costs by going home less frequently. There are four major breaks during the academic year: Thanksgiving break, winter break, spring break and summer break. Traveling to and from home (and vacationing on spring break) can add thousands of dollars to college costs.

Do not charge more than you can afford to pay off in-full each month. If you carry a balance on your credit cards, you are living beyond your means.

Parking on college campuses can be very expensive. Parking spaces are hard to find, as the campus parking lots are often oversold.

Do not spend money in vending machines.

Even innocuous expenses, like eating out and buying food from vending machines, can quickly add up. Purchasing a $10 pizza each week will cost $2,000 over the course of a 4-year college career. If you use student loan money to pay for the pizza, it will cost about $4,000 by the time the debt is repaid.

A $10 pizza a week costs $2,000 over a 4-year college career. Pay for it with loans & the cost doubles to $4,000 when the debt is repaid.

A financial literacy course will help you make smarter borrowing decisions in college. Financial literacy training will also help you become more successful after you graduate by teaching you how to manage your money.

May

May 1 is the National Candidates Reply Date, also known as College Decision Day. Students must accept offers of college admissions by this date.

May 29 (5/29) is National College Savings Day. See also September, which is National College Savings Month.

The Intel International Science and Engineering Fair (ISEF) is held in May. Visit https://student.societyforscience.org/intel-isef for more information.

Before Saving for College and/or Retirement

Build an emergency fund of 3-6 months' salary and keep it in a liquid investment, where you can access the money quickly. This is usually enough money to cover living costs between jobs, should you become unemployed.

Why Save for College?

It is cheaper to save than to borrow. If you save $200 a month for 10 years at 6.8% interest, you will accumulate $34,433. If instead of saving, you borrow $34,433 at 6.8% interest with a 10-year repayment term, you will pay $396 a month, almost twice as much. When you borrow, you *pay* the interest; when you save, you *earn* the interest.

Children who have college savings plans are more likely to enroll in college. It sets up an expectation that the child will go to college.

Saving for college gives the student greater flexibility in college choice. Having a college savings plan allows the student to choose a more expensive college.

When to Start Saving for College

Start saving for college as soon as possible. Time is your greatest asset. If you start saving for college at birth, about a third of your college savings goal will come from the earnings. If you wait until the child enters high school, less than 10% of the savings will come from earnings.

The sooner you start saving for college, the more time you'll have for your investment returns to compound.

It is never too late to start saving. Every dollar you save is about a dollar less you will have to borrow. Every dollar you borrow will cost you about two dollars by the time you repay the debt. So, even if you start saving late, every dollar you save will save money.

How Much to Save for College

Most people do not save enough for college. You should aim to save at least one-third of future college costs.

1/3 Rule: Like any lifecycle event, the net price of college will be spread out over time. About one-third of future college costs will come from past income (savings), about one-third from current income and about one-third from future income (loans).

College costs triple in the 17 years from birth to college enrollment.

Combining the 1/3 rule with college costs tripling from birth to matriculation suggests that the college savings goal should be the full cost of a college education the year the child was born.

For a baby born this year, save $250 a month if the baby will enroll in an in-state public college, $400 a month for an out-of-state public college and $500 a month for a private non-profit college.

How to make it Easier to Save for College

Set up automatic monthly transfers from your bank accounts to a college savings plan, so you don't have to take extra steps each month to save.

There are 529 college savings plans where you can set up an automatic monthly transfer of as little as $25 a month.

Increase college savings plan contributions whenever regular expenses like diapers and daycare end.

College Savings Strategies

When setting up a savings plan, minimizing costs is the key to maximizing returns.

When choosing a college savings plan, consider the plans with the lowest fees. Minimizing costs is the key to maximizing net returns. Look for plans that charge less than 1% in fees. The fees on the direct-sold version of a state's 529 college savings plan are usually much lower than the fees on advisor-sold plans.

Also, consider your own state's college savings plan, if your state offers a state income tax deduction or state income tax credit on contributions to the state's plan.

Thirty-four states and the District Columbia offer a state income tax deduction or state income tax credit on contributions to the state's 529 college savings plan. Consider your own state's 529 plan in addition to the 529 plans of the states with the lowest fees. Getting a state income tax benefit is like receiving a discount on tuition and other college costs. It is especially beneficial when the student will be enrolling in college soon or when the student is already enrolled in college.

When choosing a 529 college savings plan, low fees are more important that state income tax deductions when the child is young, since the state income tax benefits are based on a single year's contributions while the fees are charged annually on the full value of the investment.

When comparing the impact of fees with the state income tax deduction, compare the marginal state income tax rate with the product of the difference in fees and the number of years until college matriculation. If the tax rate is lower, investing in the plan with the lower fees will generally yield a greater net return on investment.

Save in the parent's name, not the student's, as this will reduce the impact on eligibility for need-based financial aid. Parent assets are not assessed as severely as student assets. At most, 5.64% of the net worth of the parent assets will be counted toward the expected family contribution (EFC), compared with 20% of student assets. The main exception is college savings plans: A dependent student's 529 college savings plan is treated as though it were a parent asset.

College Savings Investment Strategies

Evaluate investments annually. Review investment performance at least once a year and, if necessary, change the specific investments or investment strategy.

Review your college savings plan's asset allocation every year, especially if you are not invested in an age-based asset allocation.

Diversify investments by investing in a broad-based index fund, such as an S&P 500 index, a total stock market mutual fund or an Exchange-Traded Fund. Such investments mirror the performance of the stock market as a whole, reducing the risk of big losses from a single stock pick.

Dollar-cost averaging is a reasonably effective investment strategy. With dollar cost averaging, the parent invests the same dollar amount each month, regardless of the performance of the stock market. When prices are low, this strategy purchases more shares. When prices are high, it purchases fewer shares. It is similar in concept to the strategy of "buy low, sell high."

Age-Based Asset Allocation

Use an age-based asset allocation to minimize the risk of loss in 529 college savings plans. This strategy starts off with an aggressive mix of investments when the child is young and less money has been accumulated. As college approaches, shift to a more conservative mix of investments, where there is no risk of loss to principal. When college matriculation is imminent, no more than 20% of the portfolio should be invested in stocks, REITs, options, hedge funds, bonds or other risky investments. Use more conservative investments for the remaining 80% of the college savings plan's portfolio as the student nears college enrollment.

By the student's junior year in high school, most of the money in the student's college savings plan should be in low-risk investments where there is little or no risk of loss.

Types of College Savings Plans

Consider using a 529 college savings plan to save for college, since 529 plans provide significant tax and financial aid benefits for college savings.

If you expect your income to increase significantly by the time your child enrolls in college, it may be worthwhile to sell your Series I and Series EE U.S. Savings Bonds now, to roll the proceeds into a 529 college savings plan, while your income is still eligible for the exclusion from income on the interest on these bonds.

To reduce the impact of an UGMA or UTMA account on student aid eligibility, roll the money into a custodial 529 college savings plan, where the student is both account owner and beneficiary. Such a custodial 529 plan will be reported on the FAFSA as though it were a parent asset, yielding more favorable financial aid treatment.

Wait until after filing the FAFSA for the student's senior year in college to take a tax-free return of contributions from a Roth IRA to pay down student loan debt. (This assumes that the student will not be immediately enrolling in graduate or professional school after graduating with an undergraduate degree.)

Saving for Retirement

Most people do not save enough for retirement. Save a fifth of your income for the last fifth of your life.

If choosing between saving for retirement and saving for college, save for both.

Maximize the employer match on contributions to your retirement plan, as that's free money.

Employees should always maximize the employer match on their retirement plan contributions, since that is free money.

Live below your means, so you have the means to live.

June

The Collegiate Inventors Competition (www.collegiateinventors.org) and the Stuck at Prom Scholarship (www.stuckatprom.com) have June scholarship deadlines.

Minimize Student Loan Debt

Education debt may be good debt because it is an investment in the student's future, but too much of a good thing can hurt you.

Student loan debt is like cooking a lobster. By the time you notice the water is boiling, you are already cooked.

It is easier to reduce debt before you borrow than afterward.

Budget before you borrow.

Do not treat loan limits as targets. Borrow as little as you *need*, not as much as you *can*.

Students do not need to accept the full loan amount. You can borrow less.

Prefer gift aid over student loans, as gift aid does not need to be repaid.

Loans are not free money. They have to be repaid, usually with interest.

Loans are not financial aid. They are merely a way of financing the net price of a college education.

Reduce debt by asking the college financial aid office to replace student loans with student employment. You can also return the loan to the lender.

The higher a college's net price, the higher the debt at graduation.

College students who graduate with no debt are twice as likely to go on to graduate or professional school, as compared with students who graduate with some debt.

Every dollar you borrow will cost about two dollars by the time you repay the debt. Before spending student loan money on anything, consider whether you'd still buy it at twice the price.

Needing to borrow from the Federal Parent PLUS loan or private student loans may be a sign of over-borrowing.

Undergraduate students who borrow more than $10,000 a year graduate with more debt than 90% of their peers.

Keep Debt in Sync with Income

Keep student loan debt in sync with your income after graduation.

Total student loan debt at graduation should be less than your annual starting salary and, ideally, a lot less.

To estimate student loan debt at graduation, multiply first-year debt by the length of the education program. This will yield a result that is within about 15% of the actual total.

Don't borrow more than you can afford to repay in ten years or by the time you retire, whichever comes first. If retirement is only five years away, borrow half as much.

If total student loan debt is less than your annual income, you'll be able to repay your loans in ten years or less.

If total student loan debt is more than your annual income, you'll struggle to make your monthly loan payments.

If you borrow more than twice your expected starting salary, you will be at high risk of defaulting on your student loans.

Parents should borrow no more for all their children than their annual income.

Parents should borrow no more for all their children than they can afford to repay in ten years or by the time they retire, whichever comes first. If retirement is only five years away, they should borrow half as much.

Alternatives to Student Loans

Ask college if they offer a tuition installment plan. Tuition installment plans break up the college bill into equal, interest-free monthly installments for an up-front fee that is typically less than $100.

Tuition installment plans are a good alternative to long-term student loan debt.

Tuition installment plans spread out college costs in equal monthly installments for a small upfront fee.

Choosing Student Loans

Borrow federal first, as federal student loans are cheaper, more available and have better repayment terms than private student loans.

Federal student loans are eligible for income-based repayment and public service loan forgiveness, while private student loans are not.

If you default on a home equity loan or line of credit, you can lose your home; if you default on a student loan, the lender cannot repossess your education.

Private student loans are not eligible for income-based repayment and public service loan forgiveness.

Best loans: Subsidized federal loans don't accrue interest while the student is in school and during the grace period.

Subsidized vs. Unsubsidized Student Loans

Since the federal government pays the interest on subsidized loans during the in-school and grace periods, it is like paying 0% interest during those time periods.

The subsidized interest benefit on the subsidized Federal Stafford Loan is roughly the equivalent of dividing the interest rate on an unsubsidized Federal Stafford Loan in half.

Unsubsidized loans do accrue interest in school. This interest will be added to the loan balance when the loan enters repayment.

The unsubsidized Federal Stafford loan and Federal PLUS loans do not depend on demonstrated financial need, so even wealthy families will qualify for these low-cost federal loans.

Borrowers with an adverse credit history are ineligible for the Federal PLUS loan. An adverse credit history includes a serious delinquency, bankruptcy discharge, foreclosure, repossession, tax lien or wage garnishment.

For unsubsidized Federal loans, interest is not capitalized until repayment begins. Paying interest as it accrues or at repayment has the same impact.

If a student loan is subsidized, wait until graduation to begin repaying debt. The government pays the interest during the in-school and grace periods.

Saving on Student Loans

For private student loans, agreeing to in-school payments may yield a lower interest rate.

The interest rate on a variable-rate loan can increase significantly over the life of the loan and may ultimately cost more than a fixed-rate loan.

Typically, a borrower's credit score decreases and interest rates increase with each year in school, as the borrower's credit utilization increases.

Try to avoid paying points or other up-front fees on a loan if you intend to pay off the debt early.

Beware of Student Loan Scams

If someone requires the student to pay an application fee or other fee before he or she can get a loan, it may be an advanced-fee loan scam.

Legitimate federal and private student loans do not charge up-front fees. Any fees are deducted from the disbursement check.

Federal law prohibits credit repair services from charging up-front fees.

Cosigning Student Loans

A creditworthy cosigner can increase the chances that the borrower will be approved for a private student loan.

A creditworthy cosigner can help the borrower qualify for a private student loan with a lower interest rate, since interest rates are based on the higher of the borrower's and cosigner's credit scores.

A credit score predicts the likelihood that a prospective borrower will repay the debt on time as per the agreement or promissory note, based on the borrower's credit history.

More than 90% of new private student loans to undergraduate students and more than 75% of new private student loans to graduate and professional students required a cosigner.

A cosigner is a co-borrower, equally obligated to repay the debt.

A cosigned loan shows up on the credit history of both the borrower and cosigner. This can affect the cosigner's ability to obtain and refinance other debt.

If the borrower of a cosigned loan is late with a payment or defaults on the loan, it will ruin the credit scores of *both* the borrower and cosigner.

Cosigners should only cosign a loan if they are willing and able to repay the debt entirely on their own.

There should be a boxed warning label on loan documents that says, "Warning: Cosigning a student loan may be hazardous to your wealth."

An endorser is a cosigner on a Federal PLUS loan.

Student Loan Tips and Tools

Use the loan repayment calculator at www.edvisors.com/loan-payment-calculator/

Get tip sheets about student loans at www.edvisors.com/ask/tips

Get tips about borrowing student loans at www.edvisors.com/college-loans/

July

Financial Aid for Transfer Students

Financial aid does not directly transfer from one college to another. Instead, the student must reapply for aid at the new school.

There may be less institutional aid available for transfer students.

Mid-year transfers do not reset their eligibility for federal grants and loans. Instead, these students may obtain aid only up to their remaining annual eligibility.

Some aid may need to be returned depending on the timing of a mid-year transfer and college's refund policy.

August

Student Employment

Students can earn money for school and gain valuable experience by working part-time during the school year and full-time during school breaks.

Students should work part-time (up to 12 hours/week) during the school year and full-time during the summer to earn money for school.

Working 12 hours a week or less during the academic year can improve grades, by forcing the student to learn time-management skills.

Students who work 40 or more hours a week during the academic year are half as likely to graduate as students who work 12 hours or less a week.

The more hours a student works, the less likely he or she is to graduate. Working longer hours takes too much time away from academics.

Students who are interested in a career in the military should consider ROTC scholarships.

Employment after Graduation

For most students, the primary purpose in going to college is to get an education and to get a good job after graduation.

Bachelor's degree recipients pay more than double the federal income tax of people who have just a high school diploma.

The Challenge of Developing Effective Twisdoms

Although twisdoms seem simple in hindsight, a matter of common sense, they often require a lot of effort and careful analysis to develop. For example, although it may seem obvious that total student loan debt at graduation should be less than the borrower's annual starting salary, the origin of this twisdom is much more complicated.

What is Affordable Debt?

For decades, advice concerning excessive debt was focused on debt-service-to-income ratios. Many people, including the author of this book, advised students that total monthly student loan debt payments should be less than 10 percent of gross monthly income, with a stretch limit of 15 percent of monthly income. The 10 percent threshold appeared in internal U.S. Department of Education reports. (The use of percentages of income is similar in concept to the credit underwriting criteria used by mortgage lenders, which cap the percentage of income that can be used to repay a mortgage as a way of specifying how much debt the borrower can afford to repay.)

But calculating monthly payments and percentages of income is too complicated in practice for most student loan borrowers. Most borrowers are incapable of performing loan amortization calculations or percentages of income without a special-purpose calculator. Requiring the use of an external tool makes a rule of thumb less effective, because it makes the rule less immediate in impact.

One workaround is to develop additional rules of thumb, such as the monthly payment on a student loan being about one percent of the original loan balance, assuming a 10-year repayment term. So, to calculate the monthly payment, remove the two least significant digits from the amount borrowed. For example, this rule of thumb would suggest that the monthly payment on a $35,000 student loan is about $350 on a 10-year repayment term. With an interest rate of 4.66%, the actual monthly payment is $365.

Yet, each added step reduces the likelihood that a consumer will rely on the rule of thumb. Ideally, a rule of thumb should be self-contained, without requiring additional steps or insights to implement the rule of thumb.

Every component of a twisdom should be simple, relying on information that is readily available to the consumer, such as the amount of debt and annual income. This suggested that it might be worthwhile to translate the rule of thumb concerning debt-service-to-income ratios into one involving the amount of debt and annual income.

So, if monthly loan payments should be about 10 to 15 percent of gross monthly income, what does that mean for total debt and annual income?

Start with the complicated detailed analysis and try to simplify it to yield a rule of thumb.

Assuming a total loan balance of B, a repayment term of N years and an interest rate of R, the monthly payment P can be calculated using the following equation:

$$P = B \times \frac{\left(1 + \frac{R}{12}\right)^{12N}}{\left(1 + \frac{R}{12}\right)^{12N} - 1} \times \frac{R}{12}$$

Clearly, this equation is too complicated to be the basis for a twisdom, even though it can be derived using only concepts from Algebra II, such as summing a finite geometric series.

(One aspect of creating rules of thumb involves approximations. This particular equation can be approximated as $P = B\left(R + \frac{1}{N}\right)/12$ or refined further as $P = B\left(\frac{R}{2} + \frac{1}{N}\right)/12$. The latter, in turn, yields an approximation for the total payments over the life of a loan as about equal to $B + \frac{B \times R}{2}N$. One can also draw insights from the full formula, such as doubling the loan balance will double the monthly payment.)

But, perhaps we can use this equation to recast the debt-service-to-income ratios into a simpler debt-to-income ratio. To do so, we need to make certain assumptions:

- A reasonable amount of student loan debt is debt that can be repaid in 10 years or less.

- The interest rate on a student loan will be between 4% and 9%.
- The monthly loan payment is affordable if it is less than 10% to 15% of the monthly adjusted gross income (AGI).

Based on these assumptions, we can analyze the impact using the extremes of the interest rate range, since there is a monotonic relationship between monthly loan payments and interest rates.

Extrema #1: Interest Rate is 4%

- The monthly loan payment is 1.01% of the loan balance
- For the monthly loan payment to be affordable, the loan balance must then be between 82% and 123% of the annual AGI

Extrema #2: Interest Rate is 9%

- The monthly loan payment is 1.27% of the loan balance
- For the monthly loan payment to be affordable, the loan balance must then be between 66% and 99% of the annual AGI

The actual figure will be somewhere in between the two sets of extrema. To obtain a simple rule of thumb, we pick a nice round number that is close to both ranges, namely 100%. This yields the twisdom that the total student loan debt at graduation should be less than the borrower's annual income.

To make sure we didn't simplify too much, we need to test the rule of thumb to validate it.

We can validate the rule of thumb by running the calculations in reverse. If the debt-to-income ratio is 100%, the debt-service-to-income ratio is 12.1% for an interest rate of 4% and 15.2% for an interest rate of 9%, within the affordable range.

We can also validate the rule of thumb by testing it on empirical data. At the historical average student loan interest rate of 6.8%, the debt-service-to-income ratio is 13.8% when the debt-to-income ratio is 100%.

Rule of 72

Most people are familiar with the Rule of 72, which is a shortcut for calculating the doubling time for an investment with annual compounding of interest. Simply divide 72 by the interest rate. For example, at a 4% interest rate, it will take about 72/4 = 18 years for the investment to double in value.

The Rule of 72 can also be used to calculate the interest rate for a particular doubling time. To double the value of an investment in 6 years, the required interest rate is 72/6 = 12%.

There are several similar rules of thumb, such as:

- Triple an Investment → Rule of 120
- Quadruple an investment → Rule of 144
- Quintuple an investment → Rule of 160 or 168

Note that the Rule of 144 is essentially double the Rule of 72.

These rules generally involve choosing a number that has many possible integer factors. For example, 120 has factors of 1, 2, 3, 4, 5, 6, 8, 10, 12, 15, 20, 24, 30, 40, 60 and 120. We didn't choose to use the Rule of 119, because 119 is the product of just two prime numbers, 7 and 17. However, since there are 17 years from birth to college enrollment, the Rule of 119 is useful because it tells us that college costs will triple with an interest rate of 7%.

If one uses daily compounding instead of annual compounding of interest, the Rule of 69 can be used to specify the doubling time.

The Rule of 70 can be used to calculate how long it will take inflation to cause the value of an investment to drop in half. Just divide 70 by the inflation rate.

There are two main approaches to deriving the Rule of 72 and similar rules. Given a return on investment, R, and a number of years, N, the multiple increase in investment value, M, is defined by this equation:

$$M = \left(1 + \frac{R}{100}\right)^N$$

The first approach involves taking the logarithm of both sides and solving for N x R:

$$N \times R = \frac{R}{\log\left(1 + {}^{R}\!/_{100}\right)} \times \log M$$

For M = 2, this yields 71.4 for R = 6, monotonically increasing to 72.7 for R = 10, suggesting that one should pick 72 for this rule.

The second approach involves expanding the exponentiation, approximating it with the first few terms of the expansion and solving the resulting quadratic equation for N x R:

$$N \times R = 100 \times \left(\sqrt{(2M - 1)} - 1\right)$$

For M = 2, this equation yields a value of $100 \times (\sqrt{3} - 1)$, which is about 73.2, again close to 72. For M = 3, this equation yields a value of $100 \times (\sqrt{5} - 1)$, which is about 123.6, between 120 and 124. The latter has 31 as a factor, while the former involves just small prime numbers, so we pick the Rule of 120 for tripling time.

Equations

Cost of Attendance (COA) = tuition, fees, room, board, textbooks, supplies, equipment, transportation, miscellaneous/personal expenses

EFC = Parent Contribution + Student Contribution

Demonstrated Financial Need = Cost of Attendance (COA) – Expected Family Contribution (EFC)

Financial Aid = Gift Aid + Self-Help Aid = approximately the Demonstrated Financial Need

Gift Aid = Grants + Scholarships + Tuition Waivers + Other Money that doesn't need to be Earned or Repaid

Net Cost = Cost of Attendance - Financial Aid = approximately the EFC

Net Price = Cost of Attendance (COA) - Gift Aid (Grants, Scholarships, Tuition Waivers)

Selectivity = Number of Offers of Admission / Number of Applications

Self Help Aid = Student Loans + Student Employment

Unmet Need (Gap) = Financial Need - Financial Aid = Cost of Attendance - Financial Aid – EFC

Yield = Number of Enrolled Students / Number of Offers of Admission

Resources

Edvisors.com publishes several resources that may be of interest to readers of this book:

- Edvisors.com has the most comprehensive college admissions and financial aid glossary, with definitions of more than 750 terms. It is available at www.edvisors.com/glossary
- Edvisors.com provides free, downloadable tips sheets covering a range of topics, such as scholarships, saving for college, making college more affordable, filing the FAFSA, student loans and education tax benefits. The tip sheets are available at www.edvisors.com/ask/tips

Made in the USA
San Bernardino, CA
08 August 2015